20TH CENTURY AMERICAN COMPOSERS

Intermediate Level Piano

41 Works by 9 Composers

Dénes Agay • George Antheil • Samuel Barber • Paul Creston • David Diamond
William L. Gillock • Morton Gould • Alan Hovhaness • Robert Muczynski

T0079159

ISBN 978-1-4950-0816-0

ED 4605

G. SCHIRMER, Inc.

DISTRIBUTED BY

HAL•LEONARD®
CORPORATION

7777 W. BLUEMOUND RD. P.O. BOX 13819 MILWAUKEE, WI 53213

www.musicsalesclassical.com
www.halleonard.com

CONTENTS

NOTES ON THE MUSIC

Dénes Agay (1911–2007)
DANCING LEAVES (1961)
PRELUDE TO A FAIRY TALE (1969)

Hungarian composer, pedagogue, and music editor Dénes Agay received his doctorate in composition and piano from the Liszt Ferenc Academy of Music in Budapest in 1934. He also studied law at the urging of his father, who believed it would be too difficult to make a living in music. Following an invitation to conduct the Budapest Philharmonic in a performance of one of his symphonies, Agay's dream of making a career in music became more tangible. Agay was Jewish, and he moved to New York in 1939 to flee Nazism. His parents tragically died in Auschwitz. After becoming an American citizen, he enlisted in the army in 1942, quickly rising to the rank of sergeant. His piano skills came in handy as entertainment for hospitalized soldiers. After the war, Agay worked as a teacher, composer, and publisher, and as conductor and arranger for the NBC radio show "Guest Star." In addition to composing primarily educational piano pieces, he compiled piano anthologies for pedagogical purposes. His anthology *Best Loved Songs of the American People* sold millions of copies. *Dancing Leaves* and *Prelude to a Fairy Tale* are two of Agay's pedagogical works for young pianists.

George Antheil (1900–1959)
LITTLE SHIMMY (1923)

After studying with Constantin von Sternberg in Philadelphia and Ernest Bloch in New York, American composer George Antheil moved to Berlin in 1922. He travelled around Europe as a concert pianist, often performing his own works. In 1923 he moved to Paris, where he became a prominent member of the avant-garde, befriending Joyce, Pound, Yeats, Satie, and Picasso. His most famous piece is *Ballet mécanique* (1925), scored for multiple pianos, player pianos, percussion, siren, and two propellers. Due to the difficulty of executing a piece of such magnitude, it is known more theoretically than for actual performance. Antheil's earlier works were often jazz-inspired and jarringly mechanistic. In the 1940s, back in the United States, Antheil turned to a more romantic style that appealed to a broader public. He was a virtuoso concert pianist, and composed more for piano than any other instrument. *Little Shimmy* was composed early in Antheil's career soon after moving to Europe.

Samuel Barber (1910–1981)
PETITE BERCEUSE (1923)
THREE SKETCHES
Love Song (1924)
To My Steinway (1923)
Minuet (1923)

Born in Pennsylvania, Samuel Barber was a precocious musical talent who at fourteen began studies in voice, piano, and composition at the Curtis Institute. One of the most prominent American composers of the 20th century, he is remembered for his idiosyncratic, neo-Romantic style. Early in his career he performed as a singer, which may have helped him develop an aptitude for writing the soaring melodic lines that define his instrumental works. Barber wrote for orchestra, voice, choir, piano, chamber ensemble, and solo instruments and was well acclaimed during his lifetime. After 1938, almost all of his compositions were written on commission from renowned performers and ensembles.[1] Among his well-known pieces are the *Adagio for Strings* (1936), the opera *Vanessa* (1956–57), *Knoxville: Summer of 1915* (1947), and *Hermit Songs* (1953). *Petite Berceuse* and *Three Sketches* were published after Barber's death. *Petite Berceuse*, written at age thirteen, was likely dedicated to Jeanne Behrend, a friend of Barber and a fellow composition student at Curtis.[2] It was first published in 2010 in *Samuel Barber: Early Piano Works* (G. Schirmer, Inc./Hal Leonard Corporation). Barber's father published the three pieces that make up *Three Sketches* privately in 1924. In "To My Steinway," Barber puts into musical form his great love for the piano. "Minuet" borrows from Beethoven's Minuet in G Major, WoO 10, No. 2, which Barber noted in the manuscript.

[1] Barbara B. Heyman, "Barber, Samuel," *Grove Music Online, Oxford Music Online*, Oxford University Press, accessed August 12, 2014, http://www.oxfordmusiconline.com/subscriber/article/grove/music/01994.

[2] Barbara B. Heyman, *A Comprehensive Thematic Catalog of the Works of Samuel Barber* (New York, NY: Oxford University Press, manuscript copy consulted prior to publication).

Paul Creston (1906–1985)

FIVE LITTLE DANCES, OP. 24 (1932)
Rustic Dance
Languid Dance
Toy Dance
Pastoral Dance
Festive Dance

Paul Creston was born into a poor Italian immigrant family in New York. As a child he took piano and organ lessons but was self-taught in theory and composition. In 1938 Creston was awarded a Guggenheim Fellowship, and in 1941 he received the New York Music Critics' Circle Award. He served as the director of A.S.C.A.P. from 1960–1968, and was composer-in-residence and professor of music at Central Washington State College from 1968–1975. His works, which include additions to orchestral, vocal, piano, and chamber music repertoire, often feature shifting rhythmic patterns. He wrote a number of solos for instruments customarily left out of the limelight, such as the marimba, accordion, and saxophone.

David Diamond (1915–2005)

EIGHT PIANO PIECES (1940)
Pease-Porridge Hot
Jumping Jacks
The Old Mr. Turtle
Handy-Spandy, Jack-a-Dandy
Jack and Jill
Rock-a-Bye, Baby
Little Jumping Joan
Lullaby

David Diamond was born in Rochester, NY, to Austrian and Polish parents. He studied with Roger Sessions at the New School in New York before traveling to Paris to study with Nadia Boulanger. A Guggenheim Fellowship allowed him to remain in Paris until the outbreak of World War II. In 1951 he was awarded a temporary Fulbright professorship at the University of Rome, and he subsequently remained in Italy until 1965. Traditionalist music such as Diamond's fell out of fashion in the 1950s with the rise of serialism and atonality. While serialists like Milton Babbitt rebuffed the importance of public opinion, Diamond and the neo-classicists held a different view. "We've composed music that we find beautiful, that we have loved," he said. "You have to write music that will be loved. Now if that's a sentimental concept of what being a composer is, then I'm very sorry."[1] Although the upward trajectory of his career tapered off, he didn't completely disappear. In 1966, he conducted the premiere of his Piano Concerto with the New York Philharmonic. Leonard Bernstein, who advocated for Diamond's works, conducted the premiere of his Fifth Symphony on the same program. From 1973–1986 he was professor of composition at the Juilliard School of Music. He continued to teach there following his retirement until 1997. Interest in his works increased in the 1980s and 1990s, and he won the Gold Medal of the American Academy of Arts and Letters and an Edward MacDowell Medal in 1991, as well as President Bill Clinton's National Medal of Arts in 1995.

[1] Daniel J. Wakin, "David Diamond, 89, Intensely Lyrical Composer, Is Dead," *New York Times*, June 15, 2005, accessed October 6, 2014 http://www.nytimes.com/2005/06/15/arts/music/15diamond.html.

William L. Gillock (1917–1993)

HOLIDAY IN PARIS (1958)
HOLIDAY IN SPAIN (1961)

American composer and educator William Gillock wrote numerous solo and duet works for piano students. It was important to Gillock that student pieces have musical as well as pedagogic value, because "melody and rhythmic vitality are essential to compositions that students want to learn."[1] After studying piano and composition at Central Missouri Methodist College, Gillock moved to New Orleans where he built up a large private teaching studio. After twenty years of teaching in New Orleans, Gillock decided to devote his time fully to composing, conducting, and adjudicating competitions. He moved to Dallas where he composed and served as the first and only judge for the Junior Pianists' Guild for twenty-one years. The National Federation of Music Clubs (NFMC) honored William Gillock on several occasions with the Award of Merit for Service to American Music, and his music remains popular throughout the United States and the world.

[1] "William Gillock (Composer, Arranger)," Bach Cantatas Website, accessed October 10, 2014, http://www.bach-cantatas.com/Lib/Gillock-William.htm.

Morton Gould (1913–1996)

AT THE PIANO–BOOK ONE (1964)
Deborah's Song
Waltz for a Growing Child
The Missing Beat!
A Bouncy Tune
Slumber Song
Birthday Bells
Happy Birthday March
Growing Up

Morton Gould was born in Queens to an Australian father and a Russian mother. He began learning the piano at age four and composed his first work, a waltz for piano, when he was six. The title, *Just Six*, shows that he was well aware of his precocity. At eight he entered the Institute of Musical Art, which would later become the Juilliard School. His first work was published by G. Schirmer in 1932 when he was eighteen. Gould was a distinctly American presence, writing in both popular and contemporary classical styles and proving himself adept at conquering the rising mediums of radio and cinema. In the 1930s he played piano in vaudeville acts and at cinemas and dance studies. For radio he composed commercial jingles and radio symphonettes, and he also worked as a conductor, arranger, and composer for WOR New York's weekly "Music for Today" program. In 1933, Stokowski premiered his *Chorale and Fugue in Jazz* with the Philadelphia Orchestra. Gould's works were also performed by the New York Philharmonic Orchestra and the Cleveland Orchestra. In 1994 he was awarded a Kennedy Center Honor for contributing to American culture, and in 1995 he won the Pulitzer Prize for his final orchestral work, *Stringmusic*, which he wrote on commission for the National Symphony Orchestra as a farewell to Rostropovich.

Alan Hovhaness (1911–2000)

MOON DANCE (1949) from *Mountain Idylls* (1955)
MOUTAIN LULLABY (1932) from *Mountain Idylls*

Alan Hovhaness was born in Somerville, Massachusetts, and studied at the New England Conservatory with Frederick Converse. He became interested in the music of India, to which he was exposed by musicians in the Boston area, and later looked to his Armenian heritage as well as music from Japan and Korea for inspiration. A prolific composer, Hovhaness's over five hundred works include all the major genres of western art music. He wrote six ballets as well as other stage works, sixty-six symphonies, works for chorus and voice, and numerous chamber and piano pieces. One of his most well known works is his Symphony No. 2, *Mysterious Mountain*, premiered by Leopold Stokowski and the Philadelphia Orchestra in 1955. His career went through a number of stages, incorporating aspects from the Renaissance and the Romantic era in addition to traditions outside Western classical music. Despite these shifts in style, he consistently sought to portray a connection between music, spirituality, and nature. Mountains particularly moved him, and he chose to live much of his life in Switzerland and the Pacific Northwest due to the proximity of these regions to the landscape that served as his muse.

Robert Muczynski (1929–2010)

FABLES, OP. 21 (1967)

Composer and pianist Robert Muczynski studied at DePaul University in his hometown of Chicago with Alexander Tcherepnin. At twenty-nine he made his Carnegie Hall debut with a performance of his own compositions. In addition to solo piano works, Muczynski mainly wrote for small chamber ensembles and also composed several orchestral pieces. His flute and saxophone sonatas, as well as *Time Pieces* for clarinet and piano, have become part of the standard repertoire for those instruments. In 1981, his concerto for saxophone was nominated for the Pulitzer Prize. Muczynski was composer-in-residence at the University of Arizona from 1965 until his retirement in 1988.

Dancing Leaves

Dénes Agay

Prelude to a Fairy Tale

Dénes Agay

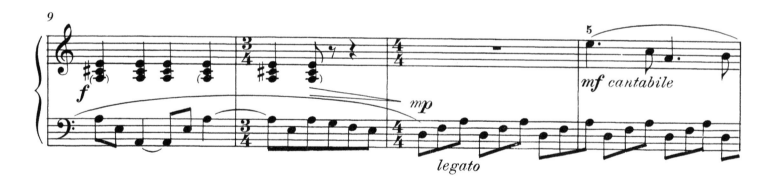

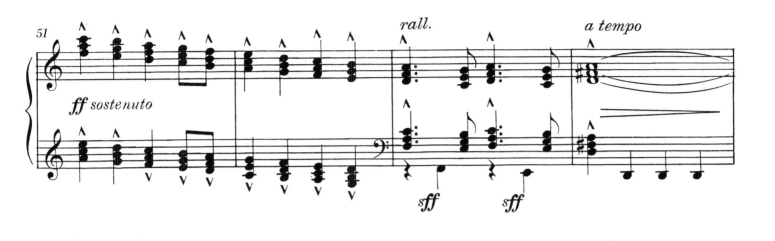

To Jean

Petite Berceuse

Samuel Barber

The fingerings are Barber's.

To Mother

Three Sketches
I. Love Song

Samuel Barber

Tempo di Valse Allegretto

To Number 220601

II. To My Steinway

Samuel Barber

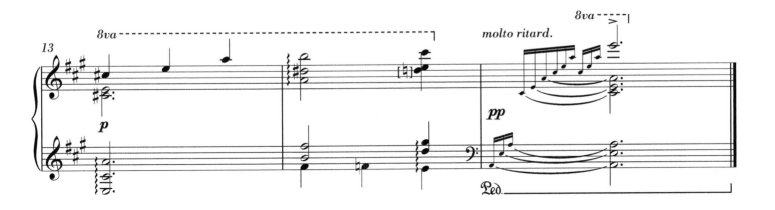

To Sara
III. Minuet

Samuel Barber

*Small-sized notes are original in the private edition of 1923.

**Theme from Beethoven.

*Barber did not indicate staccato in the L.H. eighth notes of this figure although that may have been his intention.

Five Little Dances

I. Rustic Dance

Paul Creston
Op. 24

II. Languid Dance

III. Toy Dance

IV. Pastoral Dance

V. Festive Dance

To Noal

Eight Piano Pieces
I. Pease-Porridge Hot

David Diamond

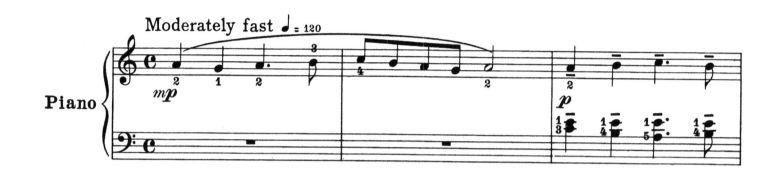

II. Jumping Jacks

III. The Old Mr. Turtle

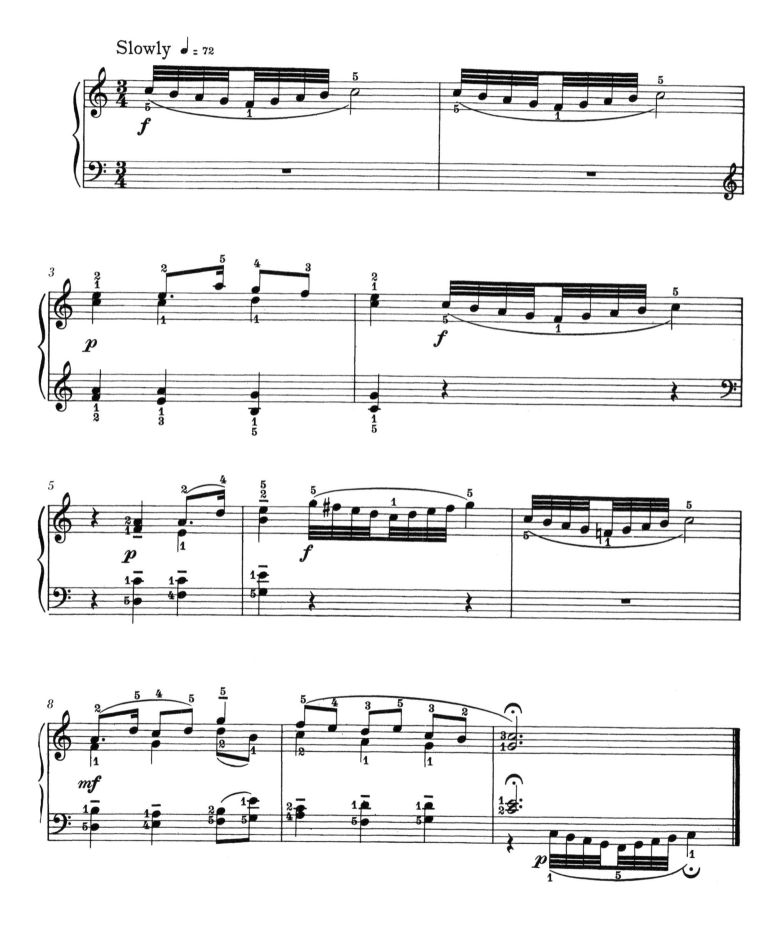

IV. Handy-Spandy, Jack-a-Dandy

V. Jack and Jill

VI. Rock-a-Bye, Baby

VII. Little Jumping Joan

VIII. Lullaby

To Samuel B. Wilson

Holiday in Paris

William L. Gillock

To The Mozart Music Club of Napoleonville, Louisiana

Holiday in Spain

William L. Gillock

CANCION

für mein nur Einziger Böski

Little Shimmy

Edited by Marthanne Verbit

George Antheil

* The manuscript does not have a tempo; this is the tempo I used on my recording. — Ed.

At the Piano - Book I
Deborah's Song

Morton Gould

Waltz For A Growing Child

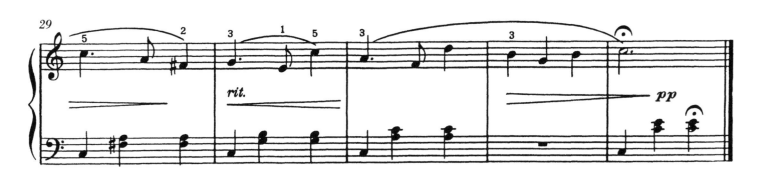

The Missing Beat!

Gay and fast waltz time

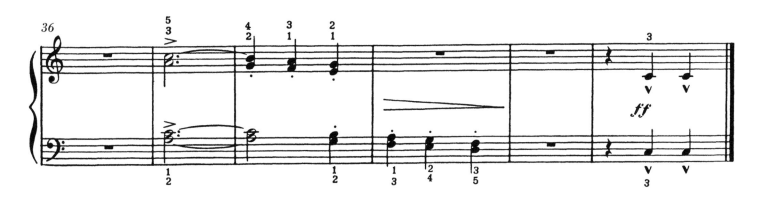

A Bouncy Tune

Slumber Song

Birthday Bells

Happy Birthday March

Growing Up

Moon Dance
from *Mountain Idylls*

Alan Hovhaness

Mountain Lullaby

from *Mountain Idylls*

Alan Hovhaness

To Mark Wansa (age 8)

Fables

Robert Muczynski
Op. 21

1

2

3

4

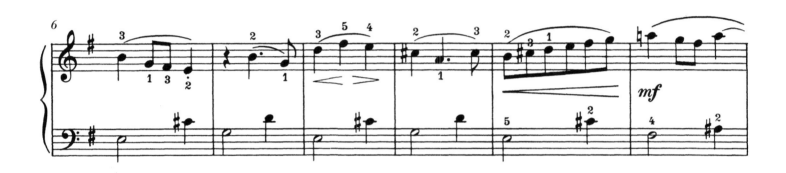

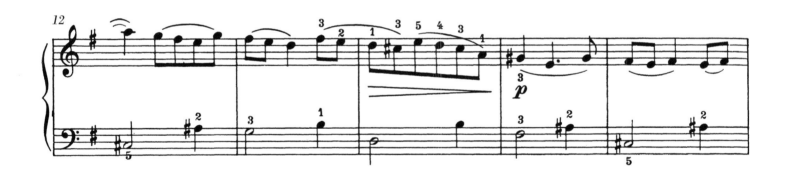

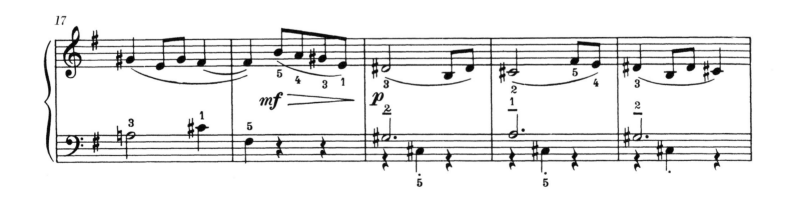

5

6

7

8

9